MW01178299

I'll admit this ɪ
told me of her n
got teary-eyed. This short book is simply brilliant, beautifully
written, and so connected to life. For me she gives detail to
what C.S. Lewis notes in *The Great Divorce*, in writing about
Sarah Smith in heaven, who had on Earth so loved animals: "In
her they became themselves. And now the abundance of life she
has in Christ from the Father, flows into them." When Kathryn
said, "I made little Charlie just for you," it reminded me that
we too were made for them, as we together inhabit this world
of His making.

—Brian C. Stiller, Global Ambassador,
The World Evangelical Alliance

Our canine friends invite us to attend on a regular basis their
"spiritual workshops" because of their unique ability to draw
us in with their acceptance, empathy, love, and playfulness,
leading us to recognize God and His love in our day-to-day,
mundane activities of life.

—Duncan P. Westwood, PhD, Spiritual Director/Supervisor,
Director of Expat Care & Development, Old English
Sheepdog owner for more than twenty-three years,

After more than thirty-five years as a veterinarian, I've found that we can learn a lot from our furry companions. In these pages, the author takes us through her personal journey with Charlie, a lovable little dog with a lot to give. Kathryn's observations and discoveries in turn give insight into God's own relationship with us.

—Andrew Newbery, DVM (Charlie's vet)

The author, in a masterful and creative way, expresses a sense that many canine owners share. Simply, that the love, grace, and mercy of our heavenly Father is expressed through all of His creation. The author has seen the character of the divine in her relationship with her beloved canine, Charlie. I love how she weaves the truth of God's unrelenting love for us through her many delightful experiences with her dog.

—Agnes Hearn, Kingdom Champion of animals, dog owner for twenty-five years

Canine
AND
THE
DIVINE

Canine AND THE DIVINE

Fresh Glimpses of God's Kindness

Kathryn Klassen
Illustrations by Elise Lu

CANINE AND THE DIVINE
Copyright © 2024 by Kathryn Klassen
Illustrations by Elise Lu

Printed in Canada

ISBN: 978-1-4866-2532-1
eBook ISBN: 978-1-4866-2533-8

Word Alive Press
119 De Baets Street Winnipeg, MB R2J 3R9
www.wordalivepress.ca

WORD ALIVE
—P R E S S—

MIX
Paper from
responsible sources
FSC® C103567

Cataloguing in Publication information can be obtained from Library and Archives Canada.

CONTENTS

FOREWORD

Jesse came into our lives on a lovely fall day in 2002. Somehow our kids had determined we would get a dog when we moved from Regina to Calgary. Neither of the adults were sure how this consensus emerged, but it had become a family truth, so we began to research the breed that would best fit our young family. Then we saw a really cute puppy. As part of our research, we asked for some details and found that this puppy was part of a litter, and there was a sibling still unclaimed. Then we made the error of going to just look. You can't "just look" at a really cute puppy and then walk away. Two adults and four kids were immediately smitten, and Jesse was at the centre of our family life for seventeen years, providing stability in transition and assisting in raising four kids.

There are many stories to be told about Jesse's role in the family. She could talk. Unfortunately not in English. When she was unhappy, she didn't bark or growl but would follow us around and grumble loudly in dog. Her meaning couldn't be missed—we had disappointed her in some profound way. After a hard day at school, she was often the one to whom kids would run to give a cuddle and to share words for her ears only. Despite this level of connection and mutual understanding, it never occurred to me to theologize about my dog. After reading Kathy's reflections in this book, I'm sure I missed much in my lack of attention to the Divine reflected in the canine.

The Psalms remind us that God's creation shouts His praise! Jesus told his detractors that if the people exalting him as he rode into Jerusalem were to be quiet, the stones themselves would cry out (Luke 19:40). We can see and hear God in the wonder of mountains, majestic rivers, and rolling plains, so why not in wonderful creatures we have in our homes and hearts? This is Kathy's contention as she walks us through a life with Charlie: from his arrival as a strong-willed puppy to the sorrow and distress of his passing. There is so much to learn along the way about caring for Charlie and the love of God for his wandering and often inattentive human creatures.

This book will warm your heart, as Kathy's love for Charlie, and his for her, is evident on every page. More than that, it will teach you about God's heart. Read this as a book of theology. In it we learn of God's care for us: how God provides and empowers our efforts to join in mission and forgives as we wander. Life with a dog has highs and lows, times of exhilaration and frustration, times of peaceful rest alongside fear and trauma. So does life with God. Kathy has masterfully interwoven the Divine and canine to illustrate God's character and to remind us in very concrete ways how God wants to assure us we are loved and known by our creator.

—Ken Draper, PhD
Professor of History
Ambrose University

DEDICATION

I dedicate this little book to my lovely little Bichon Frise, Charlie. I don't think I'm exaggerating when I say that he was a very special dog inside and out. Many said so, including the canine ultrasound specialist that examined him and called him "a sweet patient" and a "lovely dog." Charlie didn't smell, didn't shed, was playful, caring, smart, and just the cutest little cuddle monster anyone would care to have. Thanks, little buddy, for loving me so well and for bringing so much joy and wellness into my life. I dedicate this book to your memory. I miss you every day, as your personality paw prints are embedded in my memories. Thirteen years with you leaves a mark. As the little card that my vet sent me at your passing says, "I may not be able to walk next to you but know that I will forever be walking in your memories."

Painting of Charlie done by Elise.

A dog—more than an imaginary friend! More than a stuffed teddy. A real-life cuddle monster!

CHAPTER ONE

In the Beginning

ROMANS 1:20, MSG

"Open your eyes and there it is!
By taking a long and thoughtful look
at what God has created, people have
always been able to see what their
eyes as such can't see: eternal power,
for instance, and the mystery of his
divine being. So nobody has
a good excuse."

My first experience of having a family pet was in Ethiopia. My family and I lived there, and I fondly recall our little dog we affectionately named Captain. Don't ask me what breed he was. The dogs we had in Africa seemed to be a little bit of this and a little bit of that. I recall my dad picking up a pup off the side of the road and bringing it home. After a few days with him, we appropriately called him Puddles. This little mongrel would eat anything from cow patties to real food. Needless to say, he didn't live long, but we sure enjoyed him. Captain, our first dog, was friendly—at least to us. I do recall one of my childhood friends disagreeing. She had come over to play, and for some reason the dog bit her and scratched her skin right through her stockings. Unfortunately, she also remembers that I was more concerned about how Dad disciplined the dog than I was worried about her. Oh dear. Pretty hard to get out of that one.

Fast forward a good twenty years to when I was living on my own in Toronto. A friend recalls me telling her that one day I would have a house, a fireplace, and a dog. Fast forward another twenty years and it actually came true, all in that order. First the house with the fireplace, and then two years later my own little canine.

One day while up at a cottage visiting a friend, I fell in love with her little Shih Tzu, Maddi, who was absolutely adorable. So much so that when my friend shared that they were thinking of breeding their dog, I put my name on the list. About a year later Maddi had five pups. I was fifth on the list—unfortunately one pup in the litter didn't make it. I was quite disappointed. However, a week later I received a call from Maddi's mom to say that one of the four had unexpectedly become available. Did I still want one? Could I come pick him up? Off I went with a friend to pick up the little fellow. Like a proud parent, home I came with my pooch, a newly purchased doggy crate, and zero knowledge about how to raise a dog.

Yes, we'd had dogs growing up. Even when I returned to Canada for high school, we had a beautiful cockapoo named Sheba. But, needless to say, guess who did the bulk of the training? Mom and Dad! I do remember walking the little girl and comically inviting her in the winter to come out with me to make some yellow snow. But as I set out to begin training my own little dog, I realized I had zero memories of what to do. Mom and Dad had been right. They really did do the bulk of the work. I'm so glad that despite their foreknowledge that they probably would be doing most of the work, they still brought Sheba home. One thing is certain: little canines know how to burrow into little kids' hearts and leave a mark.

I was deeply grateful for a close friend who had a little more knowledge than I did about pups and who was a gifted googler. Between the two of us we set out to train this little guy. Off to the vet we went for his first visit. I'll never forget how the vet held the little pup up to his face, and immediately Charlie looked away. The vet chuckled a bit and informed me that my little dog had somewhat of a strong will. Apparently when you pick up a dog and try and get them to look you in the face, to the degree that they look away you have an indication of how strong-willed they are and what's to come.

Charlie did not disappoint. He did have a strong will, right to the end. He was also very smart and quick to learn. With the gifted skill of treat training, I was able to master 75 percent of his strong will. The other 25 percent kept me on my toes and, well, made life adventurous.

It didn't take me too long raising this little creature to find my heart welling up with love for him, and from all I could gather, it was reciprocated. I'd often hold him on my chest and pat him. He didn't purr, that's for sure, but the bond that formed was like that with a tiny little human. I'm not sure how much of his love for cuddles came from his owner or his disposition, but he loved being held right to his last days. My neighbour, a seasoned dog owner, recently confided that she'd never seen a dog cuddle like Charlie.

Shortly into this journey, I began to have these little canine/divine revelations. Don't get me wrong—I'm not saying God is a dog, or vice versa. But as my heart became intertwined with this little canine, I'd be reminded of various things I'd learned about God, only they were coming to me with deeper, richer meaning. It was almost like I was being discipled by this little animal. Before you put this book down thinking I'm completely bonkers, let me defend myself. In the Bible, it says that since the creation of the world God's invisible qualities, his eternal power and divine nature, are clearly visible and understood from what has been made. It goes on to say that no one can really say there isn't a God, because if they're really looking, they'll catch fresh glimpses of him in his creation (Romans 1:20). It's like an artist; you can see aspects of who they are in their paintings.

There's a mystery and majesty in life that we often miss. Veiled within every fibre of creation is a fingerprint of the Divine. Perhaps this is why animal documentaries are so fascinating. In a way, it's like "looking for Waldo," only so much richer. As the French novelist Marcel Proust is often quoted, "The voyage of discovery is not in seeking new landscapes, but in having new eyes."[1] The more you look, the more you see. You don't see the

---

[1] This popular quote is a paraphrase translation of a longer quotation from volume 5 of Proust's *À la Recherche du temps perdu.* See Marcel Proust, *In Search of Lost Time Volume 5: The Captive and The Fugitive,* trans. C. K. Scott Moncrieff and Terrence Kilmartin (New York: The Modern Library, 1999), 277.

same thing that you saw before, but something deeper, fuller, a breathtaking hue of glory. The more you gaze, the more you behold of the wonderment of creation—the mystery and the majesty behind it all. The mere enjoyment of our canine world can become a key to unlock fresh wonder, mystery, and the majesty of our creator coming into plain view for those who seek. The mystery is that even if we don't recognize him as such, he is still there waiting to be relished.

At times these little canine revealed truths were so real I had to share them, first with friends, and then I even snuck a few illustrations into my sermons. Truth is, they went over quite well. There are pet lovers in every crowd, and somehow dog stories have a way of unlocking their hearts like nothing else. One day a friend introduced me to an adorable book entitled *The Boy, the Mole, the Fox and the Horse* by Charlie Mackesy.[2] It's a lovely little book, an inspiring allegory filled with beautiful accompanying sketches. It really is a must-read, a book you can give to a friend or relative when you're at a loss to know what to give for Christmas or their birthday. Off and on the thought of putting some of my little canine revelations in a book would cross my mind. I loved the idea of including illustrations and, well, here you have it in your hands—*Canine and the Divine*.

Charlie made it through his thirteenth birthday. Then one day very abruptly he succumbed to some internal problems, and to this day we don't really know the full diagnosis. He had his share of digestion issues, teeth problems, and bladder

---

[2] Charlie Mackesy, *The Boy, the Mole, the Fox and the Horse* (New York: HarperCollins, 2019).

stones. One day it was too much for him, and I had to make the difficult decision to put him down. The most encouraging word I received in those days was from a fellow dog-loving friend: "Charlie's mission is over." Somehow that settled in my spirit, and I knew it to be true. He'd certainly had a mission in my own life, which I will expand on in the book, but he also ministered love to so many, some of whose stories will also be captured here.

I don't post much on Facebook, but because Charlie had touched so many I felt I owed it to them and to him to let them say goodbye. I posted a few pictures of him for others to reminisce over. A few weeks after Charlie's passing, I went to visit some friends and their seventeen-year-old daughter presented me with a beautiful painting of my little dog. Tears welled up in my eyes. It was so real, like he was popping his cute little wet nose right through the canvas. I grabbed the painting and gave his little black nose a kiss. It's the painting in the dedication. The artist's name is Elise Lu. Elise agreed to join me in this little endeavour and has done all the sketches you find in this book. What a lovely, talented artist. Thanks so much, Elise. You have been key in making these memories and revelations come alive!

So why am I really writing this book? Partly to remember and reminisce. But more importantly, the real purpose of this book is to highlight the incredible connection humans can have with creation. Yes, we all love the lake, a good beach boardwalk, and a quiet saunter in the woods. But pet lovers will tell you that a deep bond forms between a pet and its owner. As you lean into this connection, if you're really looking, you may also catch little glory glimpses of your friendly pet's creator.

If you've picked up this book, you're either doing it to humour me, or you most likely have a canine or furry friend of your own. My desire is that your heart would be warmed with the Charlie tales and perhaps rustle up memories of your own furry friends. Our creator made these beautiful creatures for us to enjoy. The mystery and majesty of it all is that as we enjoy them, we somehow get fresh glimpses of the one who made them. We see his love, his playfulness, his care. We get fresh glimpses of how deeply loved we all are.

Gently testing the waters!

CHAPTER TWO

Come, Follow Me

PSALM 73:25, NLT

"Whom have I in heaven but you?
I desire you more than anything
on earth."

When was the last time you referenced someone as "following you around like a puppy dog"?' We don't often feel the weight of these colloquialisms until we experience them. When one has a dog, this little truth comically comes alive. I recall when I first got my little guy. While crate training, I was told to put a little alarm clock in his crate when I covered it at night and tucked him in, the old kind of clock with hands that make a ticking noise. This would remind him of his mother's heartbeat, which he would have grown accustomed to in the womb. Actually, when you think of it, if you're part of a litter of five, it must have been quite noisy in there—six little heartbeats, not just yours and your mother's. Anyway, I did. I think it settled him. To be totally honest, I'm not really sure, as I purposely put him in the laundry room away from the room where I slept. I knew if I heard him whimpering, I wouldn't have the wherewithal to leave him be.

My soft heart would have short-circuited the crate training in a heartbeat (no pun intended). This, coupled with the times when I'd just lay him on my chest and pet him, proved to create quite a bond and sense of safety.

Another contributing factor to this bond was that I'm single. While at times I had renters and others boarding in the house, for the most part I was the Alpha and his chief caregiver for his thirteen years. Hence it would be quite natural for him to follow me around like "a little puppy dog."

Little Charlie was a bit of an anxious dog. I used to joke that he had his mother's abandonment issues. I had experienced some infant trauma and attended a boarding school growing up, both of which left me with some anxieties and fears of my own. So while I'd love to say they didn't affect my pooch, I doubt that very much.

I began to notice that Charlie only pined for one thing, and that was to be by my side. He didn't care so much what we were doing, as long as he was with me; that was all that mattered. This was especially evident when there was a storm about. How he hated the thunder and fireworks! Those sounds somehow pierced right through him, such that he came running to me, and no matter how tightly I held him, he couldn't get close enough.

The thought crossed my mind one day as the little guy followed me around: *I wonder if this is what God longs for in us, his followers?* Jesus often called His disciples to follow Him. In Matthew 8:22, the Greek word used for "follow" is *akoloutheō*, which can have the meaning, "to accompany." We so often think it primarily means "Do what I tell you" or "I will be up front and you fall in line behind me." While there's definitely an aspect of that in the Gospels, what we also see lived out between Jesus and the disciples was the alongside, the accompanying.

Unlike my dog, if I'm truly honest, my soul often isn't content just to accompany the Divine. I want him to do my bidding and make things work out in my favour. Isn't that what praying is all about? What kind of follower am I? Am I like a fair-weather friend, who's only around when things are going well? When the going gets tough, do I wane and wander? I want him around when it suits me. In essence then, I'm using him and treating him a bit like a 911 call, a help desk. Charlie, on the other hand, while he certainly mastered the art of begging, for the most part seemed quite content to just be by my side. I marvelled. I have so much to learn.

When COVID hit, all of us quickly shifted our commute to work from the highway to the hallway. Fifteen steps down the hallway and I was in my office. I jokingly used to say to little Charlie, "Come on, little buddy, let's go to work." He would hop to it. He loved going to work. In fact, in the mornings, lazy little lug would even try to sidestep going out for a pee because he was so eager to get to work. Had he picked up his mommy's workaholic tendencies too? I had a couch in my office that he claimed as his corner. It was right in front of my zoom camera. So, needless to say, he showed up in almost every meeting. Clever Clogs! One of my colleagues, an avid canine lover, commented that the thing she enjoyed most about our staff meetings was seeing the little dude in the background.

Truth be told, I don't believe it was going to work that was the attraction. I think it had more to do with him knowing that if I said, "Let's go to work!" it meant Mommy was going to be home all day—or for a good chunk of it—and he would get to be in my presence, sound and secure. That was a good day!

I wonder what it would take for me to learn this quality. What would it take to turn me from a fair-weather friend to a faithful follower? Perhaps I haven't spent enough time leaning on his chest, bonding and listening to the Father's heartbeat. Instead, allowing my abandonment issues to spill over into a mistrust, I've often moved into a self-protective posture of jumping to conclusions, believing that he really is out to get me or take the fun out of life. Instead of trying to use Jesus for my ends, what would it look like for me to just be with him?

Of course, Charlie never suffered. There were always treats afoot, and frequent cuddles. I wonder how much I've missed out on by keeping the Divine at arm's length. Could it be true that if I really did take more time to bond with him, my fears would dissipate? Is it possible that all my little heart really needs to feel safe is to accompany the Divine with puppy-like trust, instead of demanding that my needs get met?

REFLECTIVE PRAYER

O Divine One, thanks for creating for me my own little canine tutor. Who would think that this little guy could carry in his DNA lessons on divinity? Yet, being made by the creator, Charlie does, true to form, mirror the Divine in some small ways. Thank you, Lord, for this little gift. You know what a slow learner I am. The beauty of this little tutor is that he is a live-in. In fact, I couldn't shake him off if I tried... not that I want to. He is a daily reminder to me of you! As I watch him absurdly following me around, a mere human with inextricable faults, I long to harness just an ounce of his beautiful trait of loyalty.

The mystery is that you invite me to follow you. I've never asked Charlie to follow me. As I have cared for him, he's just adopted me. Is there a deeper truth even here? It would seem in the following, the accompanying, is where Jesus' disciples learned that He was faithful despite their wobbles. In the end, when everyone else is vanishing, they're the ones who state quite boldly that they aren't going anywhere: "*Lord, there is no one else that we can go to!*" (John 6:68a, CEV).

Hard to know who is treating whom!

CHAPTER THREE
My Provider

MATTHEW 7:11

*"If you, then, though you are evil,
know how to give good gifts to your
children, how much more will your
Father in heaven give good gifts to
those who ask him!"*

It didn't take long for Charlie to figure out where his treat cupboard was. Of course, in any normal person's house, you don't move stuff around. You usually keep it in one place. Well, the little guy quickly clued in, such that he didn't wait for treats to be offered but decided he would get ahead of the game. He'd frequently go stand in front of his treat cupboard, stare at me, and then look back at his cupboard. Dogs are not dumb. On top of this very visible gesture, he also adopted his own cacophony of sounds, each of which translated into a different demand. There was the quiet whine that I grew to learn meant "I don't want to bother you, but if you wouldn't mind." This was what he usually did when his water dish was empty and he needed a drink. His polar opposite was the definite loud, masterful bark, which was more of a forthright "Get over here right now! I have business to attend to. *Please*!"

Of course, the treats came out in the early days for behaviour modification, and they were quite effective. It didn't take him long to learn that if he stayed seated in his bed while we were eating, at the end of the meal he'd get a treat. Or if he twirled a certain way, or rolled on the floor, or did some silly thing, we would laugh and give him exactly what he wanted—a treat.

I don't consider myself a tough disciplinarian, but neither do I consider myself a pushover. Needless to say, every time the little guy sat in front of the treat cupboard, my little heart melted. I would acquiesce 75 percent of the time. The only time I couldn't was when he was ill or in recovery from some canine surgery, or if he'd already had his fair share. Otherwise, his little tactic was foolproof.

As I would stand there and watch him, I never felt annoyed with his earnestness. I actually found it quite comical and endearing. I wanted to give him a treat. Safe to say, rarely was one treat enough. When Aunt Lisa would come to visit, she loved to sit with him on the floor and pull out about four different bags of treats and then ask him to indicate which he preferred. I'm pretty sure he never caught on, but he seemed to love the opportunity to put his little nose into each bag and take a sniff.

Numerous times as I stood there grinning, a verse from the Bible would start wafting through my thoughts: "*If you, then, though you are evil, know how to give good gifts to your children, how much more will your Father in heaven give good gifts to those who ask him!"* (Matthew 7:11). Every time this brushed across my heart I'd be caught off guard. You are so right—I do want to bless this little guy. He isn't my flesh and blood, but everything in me wants to grant his little heart's desire. In fact, it actually gives me pleasure to do so. I loved the way he'd just sit there and wait. It was no secret what he was after. He wasn't trying to trick me. He was in my face with his ask. And it was no secret that he'd be back every chance he got to get more—and somehow it swelled my heart every time.

Could the Divine really be this caring? Does he really want me to come to him with this same kind of eager expectation and repetition? Why do I have such a hard time believing that the eternal, all-loving Father in heaven would feel the same way when I ask for something? His Word does say to ask and that we shall receive. As a pet owner, if it wasn't good for Charlie, I did not oblige. I'm sure Charlie didn't understand, but it never kept him from begging, and I never tired of his asking. Although it didn't work for him every time, he always came back for another go. Why then do I think that the heart of God is less kind than my own, especially when the scripture says the opposite? Why is it that at times I just stop asking for what I want, or I feel I have to couch it in some kind of philanthropic gesture? If I'm understanding this text accurately, it's saying that God is even more endearing and generous than I am. He's not going to withhold blessing. He wants to pour it out.

I have to stop and wonder if I even know him at all. Where do my warped views come from? Amazing that it takes a little member of his creation to unveil the true nature of the Divine.

This little pup is also subtly revealing to me my own heart. Time after time as I succumbed to Charlie's confident gestures, I found myself reminded of what was also available to me. I loved this little tutor. So innocently he'd be going about his business, being a dog, and somehow through his puppy-ness, I caught glimpses of the Divine, not just once, but day after day, as he repeatedly got up to his antics. Even when his little ask didn't result in a receive, he'd still be back. There was a persistence that was endearing. Is this what is meant when Jesus tells the story of the persistent widow? She was to keep asking until the judge was so annoyed that he'd give to her just to get her off his back. The deeper truth in that parable is the call for us to keep asking and not give up (Luke 18:1–8).

REFLECTIVE PRAYER

Thank you, great Creator, for your patience with me. If only I could be as honest as little Charlie. How many times have I come begging for my needs or desires to be met, while all the while having a preconceived notion that you don't care, when exactly the opposite is true? What about the times I couch my real desires in some kind of manipulative trickery, thinking I have to somehow win you over? Why is it so easy for this little canine to just come out and ask and, of course, receive, while I vacillate between vain entitlement and a waning prayer life where I quit asking? Yes, the Bible says you know our needs before we ask. Yet in the same way that little Charlie's begging warms my heart, I guess perhaps my asking does the same for you. Could it be true?

Forgive me for misjudging you, for ways I have robbed you of the blessing of freely giving, and for all the times I've tried to break into the cupboard when all I needed to do was ask. What will break this cycle? What would you suggest? How do I change from being a self-obsessed consumer into a trusting child who eagerly comes to Abba Father with my needs and even my wants? Thank you for yet another creative lesson from my little canine friend. I love that you don't give up on finding ways to teach me truth and draw me in.

I might be small, but I am mighty! I got your back, girl! No fear!

CHAPTER FOUR

Spidey Senses

PSALM 121:7–8

"The Lord will keep you from all harm—he will watch over your life; the Lord will watch over your coming and going both now and forevermore."

Biologists tell us that dogs have very keen senses. They operate at a high level of awareness, especially in the smelling and hearing departments. Depending on how much of a cuddle monster your furry friend is, one might also say they are high on the touch spectrum as well. We've all seen the TikTok videos of the pet that keeps pestering his owner to stroke him. As soon as you stop, they paw you again and again, incessantly, until you scratch and stroke them where they want you to. You won't win that scrummage. The curious thing is that we're often the initiators of that drama. You start by stroking your dog behind his ears and, well, you've instigated a "thing." He isn't going to let you stop with one little scratch. No, now you have to give him the full massage that he feels entitled to, and it's not over when the fat lady sings—it's over when your furry friend says it is. Again, there's quite a playfulness and fun side in this. What starts out as a mindless expression of affection turns into a bit of a romp, as you can't help but tease them to see how earnest they really are. And let's just face it—they are!

Back to Spidey senses. One lovely summer afternoon I was sitting out on my deck reading. Of course, I have two lawn chairs set out with chaise lounge pads on them, one for me and one for Charlie. He knows which is his chair. He does his business then up he hops. While I'm having my morning reading and meditation, he does his meditation, or slumbering, or whatever he does. Anyway, this day I was doing my reading and praying with my eyes closed when, all of a sudden, I heard this quiet growl. It was the kind of growl that warns of danger, and it's a reminder to the source of danger that the one who is growling has seen and knows and is threatening back. I opened my eyes, curious to see what had entered the yard, but I didn't see anything remotely dangerous. Charlie wasn't the growling type, so my curiosity was piqued. He was obviously tuning into something I couldn't see or hear, but something he felt demanded a bit of a warning growl. For all I knew he could have been dreaming and was growling at something in his sleep. But for me this was another one of those "divine moments." Let me explain.

Once again, my little canine friend was tutoring me in the things of the Divine. God loves to speak to his children. While many say God doesn't speak to them, that actually isn't true. He regularly communes with his sheep. We just need to tune into his language, and one of his languages is canine. This particular afternoon, I was going to get a first-hand lesson on the magnitude of God's protection for me, his child. This lesson curiously enough began with a tiny, little canine growl.

Someone had recently reminded me of the story of Aslan in *The Lion, the Witch and the Wardrobe*, particularly the beautiful scene of little Lucy snuggling into Aslan's mane. If you're unfamiliar with the story, it is so worth a read or a view.[3] C. S. Lewis pens a beautiful allegory of four little children enduring a boring English summer holiday, when they stumble through a wardrobe and end up in a very different kingdom. Animals talk. Witches ride on chariots. Beavers drink tea, and, well, creatures emerge, like Mr. Tumnus—a mix of man and goat. A curious story packed with allegorical depth. Aslan is the lion, the king of the jungle or, in this case, the kingdom of Narnia. He ends up rescuing the children on numerous occasions. Aslan is indeed king of this kingdom, who rules enigmatically as he manifests his authority in self-sacrificing ways.

Back to my little patio tutoring lesson. I just happened to be meditating on the story of Aslan and how he is a Christ figure who sacrifices his life for those he loves, constantly showing them love and staying nearby. This was what was going on in my little devotional world when Charlie decided to do his little growl. No, I didn't tumble through a wardrobe. But after having opened my eyes and seeing no danger, I went back into my quiet, meditative state. Immediately I felt the voice of the Spirit nudging me to heed. In the Bible, Jesus is referred to as

[3] C. S. Lewis, *The Lion the Witch and the Wardrobe* (New York: Harper Collins, 2000); *The Lion the Witch and the Wardrobe,* directed by Andrew Anderson (Buena Vista Pictures Distribution, 2005).

the King of kings and also the Lion of Judah. What I sensed the Lord was saying to me was this: *Your little pooch just tuned into a level of danger that you weren't even aware of, and in his own little way, he was warning you. I am the Lion of Judah, the King of all kings. I am your protector, and my senses are way more heightened and acute than little Charlie's. When we're together, if there is ever danger afoot, I will tune into it way before you will. You don't need to fear. I know you're always hyper-vigilant in your self-protective mode because of all the trauma you experienced as a kid. I get that. But often you expend energy you don't need to, and it compromises your quality of life on so many fronts. Your heightened sense of danger actually works against you. You end up living in fear when you don't need to. You have chosen to walk with me and, well, it doesn't get safer than this. Not only will I pick up on danger that you won't, but as King of all kings, I'll have a strategy in place to take it out before you even know it's there. That's the quality of the protection I offer. Even little Charlie would protect you better than you yourself could. Why not give it a go?*

REFLECTIVE PRAYER

O Lord, yet again a kind little reminder that my knowledge of you is so limited. I too easily forget how grand and majestic you are. Once again you've chosen to use my little canine friend to pull back the curtain, not only on how feeble I am but on how fabulous you are. How about I start with an apology? I know. At times I'm sure you must feel that's all I do. You're so gracious and forgiving. Nevertheless, I do need to apologize for the ways that I don't believe you are who you say you are. Even more, I need to face up to the fact that I still don't fully trust you to protect me. I still believe that I have to always be on guard. How will I ever learn this? Yes, there does need to be a changing of the guard in my heart. I am tired, and my shift has gone on too long. Divine Protector, would you come and take the next shift?

Me and my cousin Konjo wanting to come in from playing in the snow. Let us in please!

CHAPTER FIVE

Kingdom Building

MATTHEW 6:30–34

"If that is how God clothes the grass of the field, which is here today and tomorrow is thrown into the fire, will he not much more clothe you—you of little faith? So do not worry, saying, 'What shall we eat?' or 'What shall we drink?' or 'What shall we wear?' For the pagans run after all these things, and your heavenly Father knows that you need them. But seek first his kingdom and his righteousness, and all these things will be given to you as well. Therefore do not worry about tomorrow, for tomorrow will worry about itself. Each day has enough trouble of its own."

While I'm sure all pet owners would agree that dogs are illiterate, they do seem to know certain words well. In fact, they know them so well that the slightest mention of them will send the dog into a frenzy if you don't immediately deliver what you've just articulated. In bringing up Charlie, I quickly learned that words like *walk*, *treat*, and *car ride* were lethal. When others were around and I discussed my plans, or even if I was in a "talking to myself" mode, I'd have to spell out the words or risk Charlie demanding immediate action. Once that little guy was up out of his little comfort zone and darting down to the door, it was pretty hard to hit reverse and let him know that you needed about fifteen minutes to get ready. Time wasn't something he understood. Now was now.

Finally, when it was time, I'd say the word: "Let's go for a *walk*!" And off we'd go, sooner than later, to saunter down the well-known path. Charlie would often lead the way, since of course he knew it well and would wait for no man—or should I say woman!

One would wonder why a walk is so exciting for dogs, especially when they've been in the back yard a few times already to do their business. For a dog, there is much more to a walk than just relieving themselves. Something about the various scents they encounter makes them come alive.

My little guy would often sit quietly on the couch in my office and just sleep while I worked. However, when it came to be 5:00 p.m., up he'd jump off the couch and come and sit right behind my chair. If I didn't acknowledge him, he'd jump up on me, letting me know it was time to quit working and get outside for a walk. He needed to get out there.

And off we'd go.

In the early days I'd think, *Oh, a little walk will do him good. It'll probably settle him down a bit. It might do me good too. And when we return, I can get back to work. He'll be so tuckered out that he'll just lie back down on the couch.* Not! No way! Upon getting back from the walk, I'd take off the leash and he'd bound up to the living room, making a run for one of his toys to initiate playtime. The walk may have gotten some of his anxious wiggles out, but it certainly didn't tire him out. On the contrary. Walks would energize him, and he'd be raring to go again.

Anyway, back to the luscious scents on the path! When a dog goes on a walk, especially a male dog, he's out to conquer the land. Most dogwalkers take their pets down the same routes, so the dog has it branded into his little psyche, so much so that you may wonder who's walking whom!

Your dog may also seem to memorize the various marking posts along the way and be bound and determined to stop at every one of them. He isn't out for a saunter; he's out to take the land! This is his pathway, and he must loudly pronounce it, through his own unique "stream of consciousness," to all other whizzers on the trail.

One day, I recall that we went out for our saunter. Well, I was out for a saunter. Charlie was out on a kingdom mission. Truth be told, if I'm wanting a real walk, one that actually stretches my muscles and increases my cardio, I don't take the dog. However, a good little gander is always refreshing.

On this day, we set out down our usual path. He wanted to linger near one particular area, but I was a bit impatient and pulled him away sooner than he was ready. He insisted, though, and pulled back, all sixteen pounds of him, which translated to quite a force. I gave in as he did his scratch-and-sniff-and-whizz routine. Then off he waddled as if he'd just won the Olympics. I had to chuckle. If he only knew! Here he was thinking that he'd claimed territory. Actually, all he'd really done was add to the scents in the park. Other canines would follow along after him and leave their own marks. Truth be told, probably an hour later his scent would be buried beneath many others.

While I was musing to myself how silly this was, I received another one of my canine divine downloads. I sensed the Spirit saying to me, "You laugh, but the truth is you humans aren't that different. You march around claiming your territory, believing that your efforts are making a huge difference, and that it's all about you. In actual fact, much of what you do isn't that different than little Charlie here. You insist on getting credit for various things. It's super important to you that others not only listen to your ideas but heed them and then give you the credit. All the while, the world is marching along, quite ignorant of your little world."

I'm a pastor, and at the time I was working in a multi-cultural church of about four hundred to five hundred people. I'm not sure if you've ever been deeply involved in a church community before, but let me enlighten you. Bottom line: it's like a huge extended family that comes with all sorts of life and love and, of course, some squalor. While there's lots of good, there's also some not so good, including misunderstandings and distortions, and pain and mess.

One day while standing in the grocery line, I found myself weighed down and fully engulfed in my own little church kingdom world, when it suddenly dawned on me: I bet no one else in this line even knows that my church exists. *Here I am completely consumed with it, yet in the scheme of things, it's not even on the map for most people in this store.* That was a bit of an eye opener. Truth be told, I'm not all that different than my little pooch.

As I lingered in this comical truth, more revealing came. Just like I don't yell at my dog for wanting to do his scratch and sniff, but I actually get a little chuckle out of it all, I sensed my heavenly Father having his own little chuckle over my kingdom-conquering efforts. Of course, it grieves his heart when he sees me giving my life to selfish pursuits that tire me out and often detract from the abundant life he created me for. We are made for so much more than ladder-climbing and personal kingdom-building. Those things don't satisfy. God's plan for his children is for them to drink deeply of the life they've been given while gradually finding their creator to be their true source of happiness. He is the source of abundant life, not our personal petty pursuits.

Yet even here his kindness overrules. I let Charlie have some rope, enough to wander freely, but not enough to hang himself. Perhaps God does the same for me. He watches me insist to do it my way, and, well, my way is often not the best way. He keeps walking with me, despite my aimless pursuits. He promises to be with me all the time, and to never leave me, and to even protect me and rescue me out of my messes. He patiently waits

31

for me to take my cues from Him when He gently tugs on the leash, but he doesn't butcher me when I dawdle off on my own little rant.

REFLECTIVE PRAYER

Thanks, Divine One, for your gentleness. Thanks for not being one that tugs hard on the leash, forcing me to always do it your way. I love that you enjoy our walks, and that you get chuckles out of my own "scratch and sniff" attempts to leave my mark. I so often think you are angry and upset at me, and while I'm sure you're at times disappointed with my choices, you never stop loving me. I may think that the mark I'm leaving is so important, but you don't scold me for it. Even more bizarre is that you invite me to partner with you in your kingdom pursuits, which are magical and mystery. You invite me to ask you for guidance and wisdom, while also lovingly trusting me to make decisions, fully aware that I'm quite limited and easily distracted, like those sheep that stray and go their own way. And even then you leave the ninety-nine and come after the one because you actually do love your little sheep, even more than I love my little pup. Magical, mysterious, and wonderful all wrapped into one!

Can I hold the leash, please, please! I love to walk Charlie!

CHAPTER SIX

Free Will

1 CORINTHIANS 13:7–8A

"[Love] always protects, always trusts, always hopes, always perseveres. Love never fails."

There's a line in an old hymn that goes like this: "Prone to wander, Lord, I feel it, prone to leave the God I love." When one sings it, if your heart is somewhat self-aware, you know how real what you're singing is, while also being gravely absurd. Why would anyone want to leave one they love and one that loves them to eternity and back? While little Charlie loved to wander, especially in his early days, the last thing on his mind was to leave me. I was his rock, his anchor, his mainstay, at the very least the giver of great treats. I want to believe it was more than that.

A fellow pet owner gave me Alexandra Horowitz's book, *Inside of a Dog*.[4] She summarized it as follows: Horowitz suggests that while we would love to think our dog is so smart and loves us to bits, he really has just masterminded our tones and figured

---

[4] Alexandra Horowitz, *Inside of a Dog: What Dogs See, Smell, and Know* (New York: Scribner, 2010).

out how to manipulate us. I have to admit I found that thought ungratifying. I'm sure my little guy really loves me… doesn't he? Although, if I'm honest, manipulation does certainly seem to be a canine's second nature. Actually, as humans we aren't too far behind. In fact, to be fair to the little ones, our dogs are actually less rebellious and misbehaved than we are. I recall the late Rev. Timothy Keller making this point in a sermon I listened to a while back. Keller even suggested that we need to apologize to our dogs, for it's our proneness to wander that has been the catalytic cause of any of their canine mischief. This would align with the Apostle Paul's words to the Romans: "*For the creation was subjected to frustration, not by its own choice, but by the will of the one who subjected it …*" (Romans 8:22).

Unless you're living on a farm or have acres of free land, you always have a leash on your dog, or at least are supposed to. It's law in most towns. Why would you need a leash? Because like it or not, the little canines love to wander off.

Soon after getting my little pup, I purchased one of those retractable leashes. A retractable leash has this lovely little spring in it so that your dog can have a little bit of freedom to wander but you still have the reigns and can pull him in at anytime. It makes for a much easier walk for both you and the dog. I understood after the fact that retractable leashes are somewhat controversial with dog trainers. Perhaps they give the canine a little too much extra rein when the unexpected appears, like a jogger. Nevertheless, this became our schtick.

One year I had a guest staying with me, and she loved little Charlie. She would regularly take him out for walks. One day she had a bit of a canine/divine moment of her own. As she was walking Charlie with the leash, she sensed a direct correlation with how God walked with her. As a dogwalker, you want the dog to have the full canine walk experience. Your goal isn't to restrict them or make it difficult. The leash is really for safety: the dog's, and sometimes the safety of others on the path. And if we're honest, we all know that if given the opportunity, dogs will walk for miles, and not every walker has all day. Anyway, my guest found herself musing about how God's desire in walking with us and giving us some boundaries through scriptural guidelines was not for the purpose of spoiling our fun, as many tend to think, but rather to protect us. She felt that God had her on a retractable leash of sorts that gave her freedom to go for a gander, yet kept her close. He didn't want to lose her. I like that!

I think we can take it one step further. God knows we're prone to wander, and while he's given us guidelines to live by to stay out of the fray, as it were, I think it's safe to say that he doesn't put a leash on us at all. Instead, he gives us free reign, or what philosophers and theologians have coined "free will." As a human, you have complete freedom to do whatever you want. No one is restricting you. Yes, there are laws in the land that are best to be kept for all involved, but you're not obligated to do so. The only time you're really restricted is if you've broken one and been caught. Then you find yourself restricted, and it's often not too retractable. Even if we don't get caught, the consequences do catch up to us and bring their own confinement.

God designed it this way. He doesn't want robots or slaves. He's only into free-will lovers. He wants us pursuing him because we want to, not because we have to or are afraid not to. Even in Genesis 3, when we see Adam and Eve abusing their free will, it's not taken away from them. Does God actually not care about us? Even the Ten Commandments were given not to restrict but to protect us so that we could live a vibrant life. They were given to pave the way for a Saviour who could follow them, a second Adam who would come collect us from our wanderings and set us back on the path. As we've already mentioned, when Jesus does come, he doesn't demand that his disciples follow him, but rather he invites them to do so. He also doesn't chase after them if they insist on leaving.

Granted, if canines could talk, they'd tell you they hate the leash. Who loves a good yank at the throat? We put that leash on there for us. We don't want to lose our dog! We want to keep him. There are owners who have spent hours training their dog, and they master that wandering instinct so that the dog stays by their master's side no matter what. Hopefully that training is reward-motivated and not punishment-based. It's possible to train up a dog with fear and anger and he won't leave your side. But is that what you really want?

God will never do that with us. He never motivates with fear or guilt or punishment. He motivates with love—a love that is foreign to us. His love always believes, always trusts, always perseveres, and always hopes. This love is irresistible and endears us to him. Many have settled for much less. Their faith is more of a leash of rules and regulations that often hinders them from getting close to the master. The master eagerly desires to set us free so that we may live in love and not be leashed out of fear and guilt.

While on the front end of training Charlie, I kept him leashed. I carried treats in my pocket and in safe places I would take him off the leash and let him wander. When he went too far, I cajoled him back with his treat of choice. Over time, I never had to take the treats anymore. We figured out a safe rhythm and enjoyed a free-flowing walk. When I saw strangers or dogs coming down the path, I would leash him up. I wasn't that good of a trainer, and Charlie wasn't that good of a dog. But for the most part, we found our way.

REFLECTIVE PRAYER

Lord, I've grown up with a self-imposed leash for so long, it's hard to imagine life without it. In actual fact, I think I trust the leash more than I trust you. You're inviting me to come alongside you and follow you. You're committed to come after me if I wander off. You're inviting me to an abundance that actually infuses me with honour and value. Why do I so struggle to take it? You know the rebelliousness of my heart, and even that doesn't scare you away. You are bigger than my rebellion, and you long for me to not just be at your feet but to wander out a bit and smell the roses and enjoy the journey. Thanks for believing in me enough to trust me, even though I'm so slow to return the favour. You really are something!

Seriously, you're putting this thing on me again?

CHAPTER SEVEN

For My Good

ROMANS 8:28

"And we know that in all things God works for the good of those who love him, who have been called according to his purpose."

Psychologists and anthropologists tell us that 80 percent of communication is body language. That's well and dandy for animal lovers until you're dealing with injury and pain. At some point you'll have to introduce your dog to the dreaded cone. What is the cone? It's this apparatus that goes over a dog's head to keep him from licking where he shouldn't. When he needs to get neutered, the dreaded cone comes out and has to go over his head to keep your lovely canine from licking their incision. They're drawn to incisions like a moth to a flame. At times it almost feels inhumane, or should I saw in-canine—after all, the dog's tongue is drawn to blood. The cone keeps them from being able to reach the incision, or in the case of mouth surgery, keeps their paws from being able to dig and itch.

I was first introduced to the cone when I took Charlie to get neutered. It was mid-winter, and as I brought him out of the clinic, with his crazy cone on, the first thing he had to do of course was pee. And so he motored over to the nearest snowbank. Well, having no idea how to engineer this apparatus, he went right for the snowbank, face-first! One has to sniff before they pee. The poor little guy's cone scooped up a whole bunch of snow, and that was that. I was horrified. Was this really necessary? I'm sure he felt the same way.

Why do I refer to it as the "dreaded" cone? One look at your pup's face when you pull it out will suffice. They hate it. At certain times I've had to put oven mitts on to protect my own paws from the little fellow's growl and grit.

Not only was the cone dreadful to the pooch, but I found it dreadful as an owner. I so wanted to explain to him why I was putting it on and how it was for his own good and would help him recover faster. Of course, my limited canine linguistic capability hindered me here. I just had to live with my interpretations of those dreaded looks he'd give me. I know we talk of people pleasers, and that's a good and a bad thing. But in all honestly, I'm also a dog pleaser. I want my dog to like me. I want to please him. I know I'm the Alpha—or at least that's what I tell myself—but I really do love the little guy and can't stand that I can't communicate my intentions to him. I know dogs are smart, but I'm pretty sure they aren't that smart. I'm not sure my explanation would have made him feel better, but it sure would have helped me.

It made me wonder if there aren't also times that I've needed to be coned in some form or another, to protect me from making a mess of things. As much as we all would love the instant prayer, on-the-spot healing, most healing—whether it be heart, head, or limb—takes time. We'll all at some point in time need crutches, bed rest, medication, or therapy. How often have you and I felt like we were being submitted to the dreaded cone? This thought has actually softened my rhetoric toward God at times. I can be pretty impatient and frustrated, especially when I want to get back to business as usual and I'm laid up in some way.

The Bible says that God is the giver of every good and perfect gift (James 1:17). Just as I know that the cone is actually good for little Charlie, I suspect there are many times that it's equally good for me. The difference is that God can communicate to me what he's doing if he chooses—although I suspect half the time I'm stubbornly not listening, or at other times not ready to hear what he has to say. I wonder how many times I've given him that "dreaded canine look" and made him put on oven mitts to protect himself from my outbursts? And true to form, he doesn't take the cone off but persists for my own good. Do I really need to know why every time? I sometimes wonder if my little guy could make the connection when he was all healed up, that the cone was really an essential ingredient to his healing? I kind of doubt it. I suspect he just thought, *Oh there she goes again, doing her thing.*

REFLECTIVE PRAYER

It's me again, Lord, needing to confess. Sorry for all the times I gave you those dreaded looks, added some expletives, and perhaps even growled and attempted to dismember you. Thanks for not pulling away and giving me my way. I so often think of you as cruel and out to spoil my fun, much like I'm sure Charlie might have felt when I limited his movements by turning him into a cone head. Some have called it the cone of shame because that's the best description of the look on your pet's face when they have to wear it.

Lord, I guess there are times when I've had to go through things that felt shameful to me, yet in some way they were actually not shameful at all. Perhaps you were inadvertently showing me how much you loved me. This will take some learning for sure. Thanks for your patience with me. I need a perspective shift. Maybe next time before I get my growl on, I wonder if you could nudge me with some insights that might help. Unlike me and Charlie, you really can communicate with me. Your book says that you're the Good Shepherd, and that you know your sheep and they know you, and also that they hear your voice. Thanks for not taking the cone off when I begged you to. You really do know what's best!

A picture paints a thousand words!

CHAPTER EIGHT

Unconditional Love

PSALM 139:17–18

"How precious to me are your thoughts, God! How vast is the sum of them! Were I to count them, they would outnumber the grains of sand—when I awake, I am still with you."

The dreaded COVID-19 virus was discovered in 2019 and shortly after the global shutdown occurred. One of the industries that did very well during this time was pet sales. All of a sudden everyone wanted a dog. Those who had discussed it for ages and didn't have the time all of a sudden had the time and went for it. That was probably one of the best things parents could have done for their kids and for themselves. I often tell people, "If you don't feel loved, get a dog." Seriously, animals know how to love in ways that are uncanny. Whether you're gone for a month or an hour, when you step through your front door, your dog goes ballistic. I'm not kidding. Little Charlie would race down the stairs and do some silly kind of twirl and then go crazy, expressing his excitement that I was home.

I used to think, *Hey, dude, I was just out getting groceries. What's the big deal?* Well, the big deal was me. I was home and he was tickled pink. Nothing could make him happier—not a walk or even a treat. I have to say that nothing makes you feel so loved as when you're fussed over, especially when there's no apparent reason. I understood it when I left him with friends while I was away for a few weeks at a time. Of course, he should be excited to see me then, but after each little jaunt to the store? Seriously? But that's how it is! Anyone with a canine friend will tell you. Unless that dog is crated, or tied up or sick, he will be there to greet you with bells on.

While I believe my friends and family do love me, I don't have anyone in my life who shows that much excitement when they see me. Yes, when I'm gone for weeks or months, people do sort of gush, perhaps for an hour, but definitely not when I return from having stepped out to the store for an errand. That's pushing it. After all, we're dignified aren't we? One day as I was mulling over this curious reality, the quiet divine voice in my head interrupted my thoughts with, "I feel that way about you every time I see you!" It caught me off guard! I had to stop in my tracks. Seriously?

Actually, that's what the good book says. When you awake in the morning, God is thinking crazy thoughts about you. It's almost like he's sitting at the edge of your bed, waiting for you to awaken, so he can do the day with you. I rarely think of God that way. I think he's probably ticked off at me and waiting for me to behave, and then maybe he'll give me the time of day. Once again it took a little canine creature to open my eyes to a truth that I'm still struggling to embrace.

I've had people tell me that they find it easier to trust animals than people. People will hurt you and betray you and, well, just be human. But animals? Not a chance. No matter how you treated them just before you walked out that door, when you return it's like nothing ever happened. You could be madder than a hatter (whatever that looks like), but when you step in that door, you're the bee's knees! You are queen for that moment and every moment after.

How that just swells one's little heart! You just have to stop and give him a little tummy rub and try to settle him down, which is next to impossible. I used to tease my friends that when they came through the door, I was going to get on the floor and do a twirl and wait for a tummy rub! Seriously! No—not on your life. I might like you and even love you, but at least I will be civil about showing you how I feel.

Perhaps what we really need isn't civil love. Perhaps what we were really made for is someone to go bananas over us every time they see us. Perhaps that's what each of us needs. We'd never admit it, but our creator knows what we need. The Bible says that before we even ask, he knows what we need. Is it possible that a dog is a human's best fried because you and I were created with a deep need to be fussed over?

Don't get me wrong—I'm not suggesting that canine love replaces human love or divine love. Your lawn mower needs gas and oil. It needs both, and you can't go without one or the other. You and I need divine love and we need human love. We were made that way. But is it possible that God made these little furry creatures to sneak into our heart because he knows how stubborn we can be about owning up to what we really need and receiving it? I've seen grown men melt and act like little boys when they have a furry friend. It's like all inhibitions disappear and they are their true little selves.

I recall watching a documentary of how service dogs were given to soldiers who had just returned from the Afghan war. These soldiers, suffering with post-traumatic stress disorder, were terrified to go out on the street or into the mall for fear of being triggered. However, they found that when assigned their own personal trained guard dog, two things happened: they felt safe, and they also felt loved. The documentary went on to say that over time these soldiers no longer needed to be on medication. Their little furry friend loved them back to health.

One of the best things you can do for your kids is get them a furry friend. They beg and beg, and often parents try to put it off as long as they can. But why? Just because you don't want to walk the poor thing? Whether you're a single parent or a double parent family, your kids' love tank needs filling, and you can't do it by yourself. But if you get them a little pet, you'll be amazed. Not only will your child be deeply loved, but the little canine will crawl into your own heart in uncanny ways.

A friend of mine, a single mom, used to call me up and ask if she could drop her little son over for a few hours. She had errands to run and needed some help with him. Of course

I'd say yes every time I was able. I loved having the little guy over. A big part of the attraction for him coming over was Charlie. He just couldn't get enough of the little guy. I'd be puttering away in the kitchen and all of a sudden become aware of dead silence in the living room. I'd stop what I was doing, thinking that I better go check on what was happening to make sure everyone was okay—as a good babysitter does. I'd peek around the corner, and there would be Charlie, sprawled out on the carpet spread-eagle style, with his tummy fully exposed, as the little tyke was giving him a tummy rub. It would bring tears to my eyes. This little guy needed Charlie as much as Charlie loved being needed—and I'd quietly sneak back into the kitchen, not wanting to interrupt this divine encounter. This little guy was getting his love tank filled up, and I didn't want to get in the way.

I understand from the counsellors I've gone to that being able to communicate what you need is a sign of maturity. Unfortunately, not many of us are good at it. But do you know what? Dogs are! They have no trouble letting you know that they want your affection and love, and they have no trouble giving it back. Is it just possible that the Divine has created these furry friends to give us a tiny taste of what he has in store for each one of us? Is it possible that he spins around on the floor every time he sees you and just can't contain himself because he's over the moon about you?

REFLECTIVE PRAYER

Wow, Lord. Could this be really true? Do you really feel this way about me? I'm finding it hard to believe, but I sure know how it made me feel when little Charlie did his twirl for me. Thanks for giving him to me! If there's more that I'm missing out on, just because I'm so stubborn or proud or ignorant to my own needs, please don't stop trying to get my attention. Teach me how to be truer in expressing my needs, and help me grow in being humble enough to receive when provision comes. Thanks so much for the little furry friends you bring into our lives to sneak into our hearts and who hug us up in their own way. I am grateful.

Anyone have a light?

CHAPTER NINE

Full of Grace and Mercy

PSALM 103:8–13 (MSG)

"God is sheer mercy and grace; not easily angered, he's rich in love. He doesn't endlessly nag and scold, nor hold grudges forever. He doesn't treat us as our sins deserve, nor pay us back in full for our wrongs. As high as heaven is over the earth, so strong is his love to those who fear him. And as far as sunrise is from sunset, he has separated us from our sins. As parents feel for their children, God feels for those who fear him."

To forgive or not to forgive, that is the question. According to whom? Shakespeare? Well, that certainly isn't a question when it comes to the canine species. They may be somewhat cautious and self protective around those whom they have learned aren't trustworthy, but I have rarely seen a human who can forgive as quickly as our little furry friends, or for that matter receive forgiveness as quickly.

I recall when my little guy was truly little—I don't think he was even a year old. We were out in the yard, and he was running around trying to chase the ball. He ran right under my feet and I accidentally stepped on him. He yelped and I gasped. He seemed to be having trouble breathing, so we immediately took him to the doggy triage, as it was a weekend. I have to admit, he was a little tentative around me. I felt absolutely awful.

We got him to the vet, and the triage vet checked him out. After issuing me a hefty bill, he sent us on our way, saying the little guy was fine. I continued to feel terrible, but it didn't take long for little Charlie to cuddle up again and get back to normal. I have to admit, right up to the end of his days he was always quite discerning when it came to playing under my feet, but his heart was never one that held a grudge or reflected any malice or distancing. His forgiveness was for keeps. Just like the psalmist says, when God forgives, he doesn't remember it anymore. As far as the east is from the west, it is done. Never shall the two meet—the offense is completely erased (Psalm 103:12).

As much as our furry friends are darlings and we just adore them, they also have a rebellious side that they seem unashamed of. Unlike humans, they aren't prone to hide it. When they choose to break the rules, they do so deliberately. Sometimes just like a little kid, they want your attention, and they know how to get it. At times I'd be working away in my office, and all of a sudden Charlie would start attacking books I'd left on the floor. As he'd start chewing up the corners, I'd catapult out of my chair and order him to stop. It worked. He got my attention alright, but not the kind he was hoping for. Crazy little guy. As soon as I snatched the books away, he'd kick into his little "let's play mode" like nothing had happened.

Every dog trainer will tell you that if there's a problem with your dog, it isn't the dog's fault. They always blame the owner. The assumption is that if your canine is overly obstinate and not responding to you, then you have failed to properly train him or her. I take full responsibility for any of Charlie's bad behaviour. When I first got him, I cheaply decided I would train him myself. If I was to do it over again, I would pay the bucks and get him properly trained. Training isn't just rewarding them when they get it right, but it includes withholding things when they get it wrong.

Just as every parent has to find the best way to get their kids to mind, so every pet owner has to find a method of discipline that their furry friend will respond to. For little Charlie, I learned over time that the best discipline was what became affectionately know as "puppy jail." Yes, I did crate train the little guy. And yes, I know pet experts tell you the crate is to be a positive experience for the dog, not a negative one. For little Charlie, it was initially not only effective but also quite positive. Pet specialists recommend you put the crate in a highly trafficked area of the house so that the dog feels like his crate is his safe place and he is in the centre of all that's happening. Unfortunately, with the way my house was set up, that wasn't possible. There wasn't a central traffic zone place for the crate, so the crate stayed in the laundry room. Before you start feeling sorry for the little guy, he did have other hangout spots, three to be exact. He was rather spoiled. He owned plush, comfy beds located in three common areas: the kitchen, the bedroom, and the office. He quickly learned all three were his, and he thoroughly claimed them as his own.

Back to the crate. It morphed into a useful tool for Charlie's momma. It became puppy jail. There were definitely times where the little guy defied me, and as he was a fast little monkey, I couldn't always catch him. How many times did he have me running back and forth around the coffee table while I tried to pin him down, often with limited success? Up until he became a senior, I couldn't catch him if I tried. I would eventually, but usually only after needing to resort to some kind of trickery, or should I say "treatery."

I will never forget the time I had a lovely lodger staying with us. Charlie came to know her as "Grandma." He adored her, partly because she was just plain loveable, but also because she loved to feed him. Well, one day our dear not-so-little lodger was outside hanging up her laundry on the line, and Mr. Charlie got a hold of a pair of her undies. You can just imagine the fun he had as Grandma tried to chase him around the yard but wasn't anywhere near catching him. Not sure what happened to those undies. When I got home, I got to hear the tale, leaving all of us in stitches.

So yes, there were these little moments when Mr. Charlie broke the rules and needed to be disciplined. He seemed to know when he messed up, although he would fight me to the end. Finally, I would catch him and put him in the crate—

puppy jail—and close the laundry door. As with most jails, confinement is an unwanted experience. Perhaps for my little guy, it was also being left in the laundry room by himself—solitary confinement.

When I felt time was up, usually after five or ten minutes, I would come in, close the laundry door so he couldn't race around me, and sit down in front of the crate and open the crate door. I'd look him in the eyes and put my hand out sideways in a kind of hand-shaking gesture, and then I'd tell him to come over and say sorry to Mommy. (I learned somewhere that hand gestures are really key for dogs. They're quick to pick up what you want from them when you assign a hand gesture to a desired behaviour.) Charlie quickly became aware that this little hand gesture was one I used to ask him to take responsibility for his not-so-nice behaviour, and that I wanted him to come over to me and apologize. I know it sounds crazy, and I haven't heard of any other pet owner doing this, but it really worked.

The crate door would be open, and though I'm sure he desperately wanted to get out of confinement, there was no way he was going to come over and say sorry. The little stinker would just sit there, with the crate door wide open, and look away like he was ignoring me. He was going to sit me out. There was no way I was giving in to this. I had to sit there and win this thing. The hardest part was not to laugh, as it was quite comical. But if I laughed, I'd lose this teaching moment for sure.

I'd stay seated, with my hand held out, repeating, "Come on over and tell Mommy you're sorry!" And he'd continue to gaze around the room, avoiding my eyes. I had learned that being an Alpha dog-owner means you have to outlast them in these little tugs-of-war. Finally, he'd come to the realization that he wasn't going to win, or maybe he was just getting bored with it all. Who knows? He'd sheepishly wander over to where I was seated, with his tail between his legs and his head down. As soon as I acknowledged him, that was it. No wallowing, no feeling sorry for himself. He snapped out of it so quickly, tail up and wagging and ready to play.

The first time this happened, I sat there in wonderment. It was bizarre that one could switch their moods in a split second. I know I certainly can't do that. But after various repeats over the years, I began to marvel. It seemed quite evident that he knew he had done wrong, or at least that I wasn't pleased with him, and once we had reconciled that little bit of mischief, it was over and done with. He wasn't holding on to it for another second. His little tail would start wagging, and he would bound toward the door, ready for the next adventure. He'd done his time and that was all there was to it. There was no lingering guilt, shame, or wallowing! He was over it and believed that I was too, and it was off to the next thing. He was free!

I found myself remembering the character of God—that when he forgives, he remembers it no more (Hebrews 8:12). As far as the east is from the west, he removes our sins from us (Psalm 103:12). Charlie was expecting me to do the same, but even grander, he was modelling how God desires His children to fully receive forgiveness and move on in great freedom.

I've certainly had my share of rebellious moments. While I haven't spent any time in jail, I have to say that when it comes time to apologize and move on, I definitely don't snap out of it that quickly. I often wallow, beat myself up, feel sorry for myself, and indulge in a few other not-so-pleasant behaviours. I'm not sure what I think I'm accomplishing, but I'm certainly not quick to leave it and move on.

In the pastoral counselling that I do, one thing parishioners often struggle with is being able to receive forgiveness, and especially to forgive themselves. There is some kind of self-centred justice system inside each of us that demands we must be right. "There is no way I could be wrong." It has to be the other guy. If we can't seem to get the upper hand on that one, then we're determined to become judge and jury until we feel we have put ourself in puppy jail long enough. Only then can we possibly move forward, but often even then with some residue of the old lingering on. In Louise Penny's fabulous detective novels featuring Inspector Armand Gamache, she repeatedly has him state to inexperienced police officers the four things that lead to wisdom that every Surete du Quebec officer must master: "They are four sentences we learn to say, and mean. I don't know. I need help. I'm sorry. I was wrong."[5] There's something about admitting we are wrong that is unnatural to us.

Well, the God I know and believe in is not one who is rebellious or makes mistakes. However, he is described as quick to forgive. The fact that he himself hasn't erred makes this reality even more surprising. If anyone had a right not to forgive, or to take his time to do so and withhold it, it would be

---

[5] Louise Penny, Chief Inspector Gamache Series (New York: St. Martin's Publishing Group). This line appears frequently throughout the series.

the holy Father. Yet of all those I know, including my little pup, my heavenly Father is the quickest to forgive.

At Easter, during Good Friday services, Christians remind themselves of the seven sayings of Jesus on the cross. One of them is, *"Father, forgive them, for they know not what they are doing"* (Luke 23:34). He is in severe pain—not from bearing the punishment of his own wrongdoings, but from taking on those of the world. He is barely able to breathe or whisper, with his chest being weighed down by the rest of his body contorted and caving in. Yet even here, he must speak out as loudly as he can to declare to the universe, to you and to me, that our sins are forgiven. He gives this freely, realizing that an apology from many will never come.

REFLECTIVE PRAYER

Thanks, Lord, for this little bundle of joy that continues to teach me about holy things. I love that you're so patient with me and do everything you can to help me to learn how to live more freely. I would love to be more like little Charlie, in being able to quickly forgive and receive forgiveness. Thanks for this little tutor. These are hard lessons, and I'm so slow to learn them, yet you so gently nudge me on, even through the comical moments of canine frivolity. Is this why they call it amazing grace?

Awww, Charlie, buddy, I have missed you so much!

CHAPTER TEN
Fear Not, For I Am with You

ISAIAH 41:10

*"So do not fear, for I am with you;
do not be dismayed, for I am your
God. I will strengthen you and
help you; I will uphold you with
my righteous right hand."*

I'm not sure where his anxiety came from, but my little canine was definitely an anxious dog. My father told me once that dogs take on the traits of their owners, so it's possible he got it from me. My dad is the one who passed on to me his love of dogs. I recall fondly him saying that when you see a dog standing on three legs, pensively, that's a sign of a peaceful, healthy, well-adjusted dog. Every time Charlie would take that pose, I would smile inside, remembering, and give myself a little pat on the back.

That said, Charlie had his bouts of anxiety off and on. One aspect of his anxiety that surfaced frequently was his fear of thunderstorms or fireworks. I'm not afraid of storms and not a particular fan of fireworks, but for some reason, before the storm was anywhere near us or there was the slightest hint of

fireworks, Charlie was already sticking to me like glue. It didn't matter what I was doing, he had to be right next to me, as close as he could get, and nothing would stop him. Truth be told, my presence wouldn't settle him. Nothing seemed to calm him down, except when the storm dissipated or the fireworks stopped. Even despite me not being able to bring him peace, I was the only one he wanted in those scary moments.

My little heart always warmed to him. I felt bad for the guy. I never scolded him. That would have been mean. Instead, I'd quickly stop what I was doing and hold him as tightly as I could, seeking to do whatever I could to help him stop shivering. A lesson on meteorology would not have helped. This was not something he could unlearn. I had a few options. I could give him some calming pills or be his calming blanket. I often used both. What I always marvelled at was that he came running to me, believing that I could fix it.

There were other times when we'd be out for a walk in the winter, and in Ontario we put salt on the sidewalks to melt the ice. I tried putting snowshoes on Charlie's little feet, but nothing would do. We wouldn't even make it to the end of the driveway and those little shoes would have either fallen off or gotten stuck in a snowbank. Yet the little guy still loved to walk and go out and do his bit to make yellow snow. I'd take him out in his winter sweater, which he didn't relish much either. Making sure the temperature wasn't too cold, off we'd go. Invariably we'd be a few blocks down the street, and he'd start limping and holding up one paw to me. He wanted me to fix the problem. I'd either pick him up, or I'd grab his paw and hold it tightly and brush off the salt. Most often the salt had gotten into the cracks of his paws and was stinging him. I'd put him back down and off he'd go. Problem solved.

In other seasons when we'd be out for a walk, occasionally he'd get a little pine needle stuck in his paw, and he'd do the same thing. He'd immediately stop and hobble over, expecting me to help him, and then after I had plucked it out, he'd be off on his merry way.

Being a "2" on the Enneagram—a helper—it always warmed my heart. I didn't have to beg him to come to me; he just did. Somewhere along the line, he'd grown to trust that I would do my best to help him, and I was his number one go-to. I never got cross with him. It was just the way it was and the way it should be. I loved being his mainstay. He belonged to me and I to him.

I've had my share of trauma in my life, and I know what it's like to have a trauma trigger. A trauma trigger is when you're in a situation that reminds you of a previous time when you weren't safe, and the fears and anxiety of the past come roaring to the surface. You can feel paralyzed and at times even quite childlike as you are stopped in your tracks. For those of us who are used to trauma triggers, we hate them and do everything we can to avoid them. The other thing we do is to begin resenting that part of us that gets triggered, and there are very few people whom we will actually trust to help us with our shakiness.

As I watched little Charlie put one hundred percent of his trust in little ole me, I marvelled. My instinct was to immediately stop and do whatever I could to ease his discomfort. That was my number one priority. Since his passing, whenever a storm comes or I hear fireworks, a part of me is relieved that Charlie doesn't have to go through that anguish anymore. I wonder if the Divine desires that we also come to him with our traumas in a similar child-like trust.

I am always in awe of how a little child will look straight into your eyes, with no hesitation. They desire to make eye contact and will often not look away. In fact, if they receive a favourable response, you've won their heart. Their natural default is to trust! Compare that with getting into an elevator with a bunch of adults. No one makes eye contact. Instead, we all either sheepishly look to the floor or gaze up at the ceiling. Over time we have unlearned that childlike trait of looking for life in another's eyes. Instead, we take our time, being on guard, and gradually dip our toes into the connecting pool, not planning on jumping in until we're absolutely sure that the waters are safe and inviting.

I never ceased to marvel at the enigma of it all. Here was my little canine friend placing his one hundred percent trust in me, one who was not fully capable or trustworthy. Yet here I am often unable to trust the Divine, who is more than capable and one hundred percent trustworthy.

REFLECTIVE PRAYER

Divine One, I know I am not as trustworthy as you, and definitely not as discerning. It's a mystery to me that I can be a comfort to this little canine in his traumas. It just swells my heart to be able to assure him that it will be all right. I know you long to do the same with me. I'm sorry that my trust muscle is so slowly strengthened. Thanks for not giving up on me and not withholding your love from me until I figure it out. I long to trust you more. Thanks for staying near and being so attentive to every little shudder and whimper that shows itself. Thanks for coming after me even when I'm hiding from you.

This is good stuff! Seriously! You should check it out!

CHAPTER ELEVEN

Catalyst for Glory

GENESIS 1:27–28, 31A (MSG)

"God created human beings; he created them godlike, reflecting God's nature. He created them male and female. God blessed them: 'Prosper! Reproduce! Fill Earth! Take charge! Be responsible for fish in the sea and birds in the air, for every living thing that moves on the face of the Earth.'... God looked over everything he had made; it was so good, so very good!"

It was a very hard day when I took little Charlie to the vet for the last time. His little tummy had all of a sudden bloated up, and the vet diagnosed that he was in serious trouble. Charlie had just come through bladder stone surgery like a trooper. I marvelled. I so hated having to take him in for these various procedures, whether it was teeth extractions or something more invasive like a bladder stone removal. He was a strong little guy, but when his little tummy filled up with fluid and the vet said it was serious, and then informed me of the devastating costs that would be involved in going to the next level of treatment, I knew what I needed to do. Not only would it be beyond my budget, but I also didn't want to put the little guy through any more pain. He'd lived thirteen good years, and he had suffered enough.

A friend came with me as I went to put him down. Only a pet owner who's had to do that knows how hard it was. The pet-owner world is a breed of its own. I have to say I really got to know my neighbours because of little Charlie. As I would walk him in the neighbourhood, dog lovers and dog owners would stop to chat and pat him. Those with dogs would gently see if their pet and mine would get along and respond accordingly. I used to joke with some neighbours that I initially only knew them as "Hamesh's dad" or "Tiffy's mom." It would take ages for me to get the owner's name because for many of the walks we connected purely at a canine level. Later, as I set out on my walks with no little furry friend, it didn't take long for pet owners to gently ask, "Where's Charlie?" Instinctively most knew, and were cautiously treading into that space.

I recall taking Charlie into the vet that last time. They set up a room with a nice cozy blanket and came in and told me how things would unfold. They would first give him a small sedative to calm his nerves and to make sure he was in no pain. Then they would leave me alone with him to say my goodbyes. When I was ready, the vet would come back in and add the remainder of the meds required to stop his heart. It was all very short and very final.

Death is such a final thing. As a pastor, I have conducted my fair share of funerals. When I would have to serve the last rites, I knew what to do. You pray and commit the person's spirit to God, whom I believe to be a righteous judge, who will do right by the person I'm entrusting to him. However, when it came to little Charlie, I just stared at him blankly. I didn't know how to pray or what to say. I know everyone talks of doggy heaven—and I sure hope there is one—but I didn't have the confidence that I have when praying for people. People have a spirit that is eternal. Animals don't. This emptiness lingered with me for days.

I left little Charlie at the vet, motionless and gone. My life was pretty hectic at that time, so in some ways I had to get on with what was on my plate, yet his absence was deafening. The mailman would come and I would instinctively wait for that bark, as Charlie hated the mail persons. How dare they touch our house and everyone's on the street, and then saunter off. Every time the mail got dropped off, it was like a cacophony of barks. He would catapult off his chair and bound to the top of the stairs, where he could see out the window down the street. Unfortunately, he could see this nasty mail person going from house to house, and he wasn't having it. He barked until he couldn't see him anymore. To be honest, it was annoying. However, now in the silence, I missed it. Every morning I'd have my Kellogg's Muselix with yogurt and blueberries and milk. Charlie would always hang around and wait until he could hear the spoon dinging on the side of the bowl, then he'd wait for me to let him lick the last few spoonsful of milk. Now I get to the end of the bowl and go to put the bowl down on the floor, and then I remember. It's all yours, girl. There isn't a little canine to finish it off for you. I miss him!

A few days after I put Charlie down, I had two words of encouragement that helped me with my goodbyes. One came from a friend. She shared that her sense was that Charlie's little mission was done. That really resonated with me. He had touched many lives in his own little way. He had helped some deal with their fear of canines. For others, he'd been their cuddle bunny when they needed some tender love and care. For others, he'd just been a bundle of joy. My coworkers loved it when I brought him to work. They would persistently try to get his attention with every treat in the drawer, and most of the time they were very successful. I recall when one of my colleagues, who really didn't care for dogs, picked up Charlie and changed her mind on the spot. She went home to tell her kids that she wanted a dog. They were flabbergasted.

The second word was one that I sensed God whispering into my spirit. It went something like this: *"People I made for myself, and I share them with you (Isaiah 43:21). Creation I made just for you. I made little Charlie just for you."* That so warmed my heart, that God would love me so much that he would customize a little bundle of fur and give him a personality that would blend with mine, and let me have him all for myself. For some reason after that, I viewed creation differently. Suddenly I had a new appreciation for what it means to be a better steward of the air I breathe, the grass I walk on, and the trees in my yard. I was sorry it had taken me so long to appreciate this.

As I bring these musings to a close, I have to say that writing this has helped me process the loss of my lovely little friend. I still look for him in different moments of my day. My hope is that as you've joined me on this journey, not only has your heart been strangely warmed, but that these contemplative thoughts would be a catalyst for you to see through the eyes of creation into the heart of the Divine.

I have to say that the God I met through little Charlie was a kinder, friendlier, warmer divinity than I expected. Not only did my heart soften toward him, but I also found that I learned to love myself more. I learned about many facets of life from my little buddy.

People frequently ask me if I'll get another one. Perhaps one day I will. For now, I will rest in the fullness of the life that we did share, and enjoy the memories as they come. It's too soon for me, but one day for sure. I look forward to owning another canine, who I'm sure will reveal even more truths to me about the eternal, infinite, triune God.

I am not crazy about cats—my bad. I've never had a horse. But I bet there are quite a few animal lovers out there who could carry on with this series. Any takers? How about someone writing *Feline and the Divine* or *Equine and the Divine*? I put the challenge out there! Any takers? Go for it and enjoy!

REFLECTIVE PRAYER

Thanks, loving Creator, for inviting me to share these musings. I do believe the thought came from you. Thanks also for the timeliness, in that it has been a gentle way to walk through my grief and experience meaning, life, and purpose in it all. I still do miss my little Charlie, but somehow to see his little life on these pages brings me great joy. I am curious as to how his little life might live on through these pages, encouraging readers to catch glimpses of glory through their furry friends, that they too may experience the wonder of *Canine and the Divine*.

EPILOGUE

Perhaps as you've read through these musings, you've felt the gentle wooing and tug of the Divine on your own heart. He never forces himself on anyone. He always waits to be invited in. If you would like to catch more glimpses of his glory and kindness, and even find fresh purpose and vibrancy in your own life, here are a few short prayers you could consider, depending on where you're at in your journey. Gently whisper them and wait expectantly. He will not disappoint!

IT'S BEEN A WHILE

Divine One, it's been a while. We've conversed before, but then life happened. I couldn't find you in the mess and, well, I moved on, not really sure you were there. I've enjoyed fresh glimpses of you in these pages. I still need some convincing that you're real and that you actually care. But I'm willing to give it another whirl if you are. You know where to find me. I'm listening!

HAVE WE MET BEFORE?

Divine One, you and I have never met— at least if we have, I missed it. As I've read through these glimpses of glory, I've found my heart softening. Are you real? Could you really be this kind? What about all the messes in our world? Seriously? I'm still not totally convinced you're real, but just in case you are, I invite you to open the eyes of my heart and understanding. I do want to see more.

MORE, LORD, I WANT MORE

Beautiful Jesus, Creator and friend, thanks for continuing to lift the layers of your majesty. The more that I get to know you, the sweeter and kinder you are. Thanks for these new and fresh glimpses. I can't wait for the more that you have to show me! I'm ready and waiting, eager and open. Come, Lord Jesus!